big
NATE
DIBS ON THIS
CHAIR

More

big NATE

adventures from

LINCOLN PEIRCE

big NATE

DIBS ON THIS CHAIR

by LINCOLN PEIRCE

Andrews McMeel Publishing®

a division of Andrews McMeel Universal

MAYBE I CAN FIGURE OUT WHAT MRS. GODFREY'S LETTER SAYS ABOUT ME IF I HOLD IT UP TO THE LIGHT.

I'LL DO IT! I'M GOOD AT THAT!

HMM... I CAN ONLY MAKE OUT A COUPLE OF WORDS... UH-OH... I SEE THE WORD "APATHETIC."

"APATHETIC"! OH, **MAN!** SHE'S **NAILING** ME!

WAIT... WAIT... IT **DOESN'T** SAY "APATHETIC"!

PHEW!

IT JUST SAYS "PATHETIC."

Peirce

COME **ON**, FRANCIS! WHAT ELSE DOES MRS. GODFREY'S LETTER SAY?

KEEP YOUR SHIRT ON, NATE! THIS IS A FLASH-LIGHT, NOT AN X-RAY MACHINE!

I CAN MAKE OUT A FEW MORE WORDS... "EFFORT"... "ATTENDANCE".. "SUMMER".... HMMM... WHAT'S THIS WORD AFTER "SUMMER"?

"SCHOOL"

SUMMER SCHOOL!

NYAA!

I CAN'T **TAKE** IT ANYMORE! IT'S **KILLING** ME! I'VE **GOT** TO READ THIS LETTER!

AFTER ALL, WHAT'S INSIDE HERE AFFECTS **MY** FUTURE! **I'M** THE ONE ON THE HOOK HERE! WHO BETTER TO OPEN IT THAN **ME?**

rip
rip
rip

FOR YOU.

THANKS **SO** MUCH.

MRS. GODFREY IS SUGGESTING THAT YOU ATTEND SUMMER SCHOOL.

"SUGGESTING"! IS THAT WHAT IT SAYS? "SUG-GESTING"?

AH-**HA!** SO I DON'T **HAVE** TO GO! SHE **WANTS** ME TO GO, BUT SHE CAN'T **MAKE** ME GO!

SHE CAN WITH THE SIGNATURE OF A PARENT OR GUARDIAN.

ANYTHING I CAN GET YOU?

A PEN.

MRS. GODFREY TEACHES SUMMER SCHOOL FOR ALL STUDENTS WHO FAIL TO MAINTAIN AN AVERAGE OF **75** IN SOCIAL STUDIES...

YOUR AVERAGE WAS **73.4**.

DANG! I MISSED IT BY LESS THAN A **POINT!**

NO, WAIT A SEC... 75 MINUS 73.4...

I'LL BE EXPECTING A SIMILAR NOTE FROM YOUR MATH TEACHER.

POINT SIX... FOUR MINUS THREE...

LEAVE IT TO MRS. GODFREY TO SEND ME TO SUMMER SCHOOL...

THAT'S **ENOUGH**, NATE!

MRS. GODFREY ISN'T RESPONSIBLE FOR YOU ENDING UP IN SUMMER SCHOOL! **YOU'RE** THE ONE WHO NEGLECTED YOUR STUDIES!

YOU ONLY HAVE YOURSELF TO BLAME.

OH, HOW I HATE HER...

I'M BEING FORCED TO ATTEND SUMMER SCHOOL AGAINST MY WILL, AND YOU GUYS DON'T EVEN **CARE**!

YOU'LL BE HAVING FUN WHILE **I'M** CHAINED TO A DESK! IS THERE NO PITY? **IS THERE NO PITY??**

GUESS NOT. IS THERE NO KETCHUP?

HEE HEE

HEH HEH HA HA HA HA HA HA

IS THERE NO RELISH?

ARE THERE NO ONIONS?

HA HEE HEE HA

OUR GOAL DURING THE NEXT FOUR WEEKS, PEOPLE, IS TO HELP YOU REALIZE YOUR ACADEMIC POTENTIAL!

FORTUNATELY, THERE AREN'T TOO MANY OF YOU, WHICH MEANS...

...**LOTS** OF INDIVIDUAL ATTENTION FOR EACH AND EVERY ONE OF YOU!

OH, GOODY. INDIVIDUAL ATTENTION.

NATE! **YOU** LOOK EAGER TO START!

MOST STUDENTS ARE CAPABLE OF DOING GOOD WORK, BUT MANY HESITATE TO ASK FOR HELP WHEN THEY NEED IT!

AS A RESULT, SOME STUDENTS GET OVER-LOOKED DURING THE SCHOOL YEAR! THEY SLIP THROUGH THE CRACKS!

IN SUMMER SCHOOL, WE WORK TO REVERSE THAT! WE DON'T WANT A **SINGLE STUDENT** TO SLIP THROUGH THE CRACKS!

NOTICE SHE SAID NOTH-ING ABOUT SLIPPING THROUGH A **WINDOW**...

NATE!

MRS. GODFREY, THIS ASSIGNMENT YOU GAVE ME IS **TOTALLY** UNFAIR!

IT'S **HUGE!** FINISHING THIS THING IS GOING TO TAKE ME ALL **SUMMER!**

SAY, **HERE'S** A THOUGHT: PERHAPS THAT'S WHY THEY CALL IT "**SUMMER**" SCHOOL!

A SARCASTIC TEACHER IS ESPECIALLY TOUGH TO TAKE ON A NINETY-DEGREE DAY IN JULY...

ANOTHER DAY OF SUMMER SCHOOL! OH, THE **DRUDGERY**!

THREE MORE **WEEKS** OF THIS! THREE HORRIBLE WEEKS! THREE TORTUROUS WEEKS!

UM... HI... I'M NEW HERE. CAN YOU SHOW ME THE WAY TO ROOM 223?

THREE WONDERFUL, BEAUTIFUL WEEKS.

UH... HELLO?

SNAP SNAP

34

WE BOTH LOVE CHEEZ DOODLES, WE BOTH LOVE CARTOONING... YOU AND I HAVE SO MUCH IN COMMON, NATE!

I THOUGHT MAYBE THAT BECAUSE YOU'RE A TUTOR, YOU MIGHT BE A LITTLE SNOBBY... BUT YOU'RE **NOT**!

YOU'RE JUST A NICE, NORMAL GUY! YOU DON'T SEEM LIKE A TUTOR AT **ALL**!

IRONIC, ISN'T IT?

HEY, HOW COME YOU DON'T HANG OUT WITH ANY **OTHER** TUTORS?

THIS IS **RIDICULOUS**! FIRST ANGIE THINKS I'M HERE AT SUMMER SCHOOL AS A **TUTOR**, AND THEN I GO AND TELL HER I'M A **DETENTION MONITOR**!

I CAN'T LET THIS GO ON! I'VE GOT TO BE **HONEST**! I'VE GOT TO FIGURE OUT A WAY TO LET HER KNOW THE **TRUTH**!...

...BEFORE SOMEBODY ELSE DOES.

HE TOLD YOU **WHAT**?

HI, ANGIE...

NATE! HI! I WAS JUST TALKING TO MRS. GODFREY ABOUT YOU!

SO... I GUESS SHE TOLD YOU THAT I'M NOT REALLY A TUTOR, AND THAT I'M HERE AT SUMMER SCHOOL BE-CAUSE OF MY LOUSY SOCIAL STUDIES GRADE...

...WHICH, IF SHE DID TELL YOU, IS A VICIOUS LIE!

HOW LOUSY?

...SO YOU'RE **NOT** A TUTOR?

UM... NO.

I **STARTED** TO TELL YOU THE TRUTH, BUT WHEN YOU JUST ASSUMED I WAS A TUTOR... I... WELL, I JUST CHICKENED OUT!

I SUPPOSE YOU'RE NOT A DETENTION MONITOR, EITHER, HUH?

ER... NOPE.

BUT YOU SAID EVERYONE CALLS YOU "MISTER DETENTION."

THAT PART'S TRUE!

WELL, ANGIE, I THINK THAT YOU AND NATE MAKE A GREAT COUPLE!

YOU HAVE A LOT IN COMMON, YOU REALLY LIKE SPENDING TIME TOGETHER, AND NATE'S OBVIOUSLY **CRAZY** ABOUT YOU!

HE'S BEEN SO TOTAL- LY IN LOVE WITH JENNY FOR SO LONG, I THOUGHT HE'D **NEVER** LIKE ANY- ONE ELSE, BUT...

WHO'S JENNY?

OOPS.

WAP!

★☆★☆★☆★☆★☆

everlovin' ELLEN!

the "life" and loves of a clueless high school sophomore!

One day at "Dilly Burger"..

ELLEN! You left the onion-ring machine on!

That's a **VERY** serious mistake! I'm afraid I'll have to put this incident in your record as a "blemish"!

I'm sorry, boss!

Well, at least I've only got **ONE** blemish!

Um... checked a mirror lately?

WHEN I ASKED ABOUT YOUR SIS- TER, I THOUGHT MAYBE YOU'D INTRO- **DUCE** US.

WHY BOTHER? THIS SHOWS YOU WHAT SHE'S **REALLY** LIKE!

63

WELL, NATE DEFINITELY HAS A GIRLFRIEND... SO WHY HASN'T HE **TOLD** ME ABOUT HER? WHY IS HE BEING SO SECRETIVE?

WAIT A MINUTE! WHAT KIND OF FATHER **AM** I? HE'S PROBABLY JUST WAITING FOR ME TO ASK HIM! THEN HE'LL OPEN UP!

WHAT'S NEW, SON?

NOTHING.

ANY... EXCITING PEOPLE IN YOUR LIFE?

RIGHT NOW, DEFINITELY NOT.

NATE, I'M YOUR FATHER. I AM **INTERESTED** IN YOUR LIFE!

I'VE BEEN THERE FOR ALL THE "FIRSTS" IN YOUR LIFE: YOUR FIRST WORD, YOUR FIRST STEP, YOUR FIRST DAY OF SCHOOL... AND NOW, YOU HAVE YOUR FIRST GIRLFRIEND!

I DON'T WANT TO MEDDLE, BUT I **DO** WANT TO KNOW HOW YOU'RE DOING! WHAT CAN YOU TELL ME ABOUT THIS YOUNG LADY? WHEN CAN I MEET HER?

LET'S DO THIS ANOTHER TIME.

TALK TO ME!

WELL, ANGIE, I REALLY APPRECIATE THE CHANCE TO MEET YOU!

I'M SURE THERE ARE THINGS YOU'D RATHER BE DOING! I KNOW HANGING OUT WITH GROWN-UPS ISN'T WHAT YOU KIDS ARE "INTO!"

THERE'S NOTHING WORSE THAN BEING STUCK WITH A PARENT WHO DOESN'T KNOW WHEN TO GET OUT OF THE WAY!

YES, THAT **IS** ANNOYING.

WELL, ENOUGH CHIT-CHAT! LET'S **DO** SOMETHING!

YOU KNOW WHAT I JUST REALIZED? **I'M** GOING OUT WITH ANGIE... **YOU'RE** GOING OUT WITH GORDIE...

THAT MEANS **DAD** IS THE ONLY ONE IN OUR FAMILY WHO'S UNATTACHED!

IN OUR **IMMEDIATE** FAMILY, YEAH. BUT WHAT ABOUT OUR **EX-TENDED** FAMILY?

HMM... I THINK DAD'S STILL THE ONLY ONE.

MAN, THAT'S SAD. THERE MUST BE **SOMEBODY** WE KNOW WHO'S SINGLE...

WHAT ABOUT AUNT MABEL?

I THINK SHE'S DATING HER PAROLE OFFICER.

SIGH...

WHAT? OH, **NO**! COACH IS GIVING ME THE "BUNT" SIGN!

I TOLD ANGIE I WAS GOING TO HIT A HOME RUN FOR HER! I CAN'T LET HER SEE ME **BUNT** MY WAY ON LIKE A TOTAL WUSS! I'M SWINGIN' AWAY!

STEEEERIKE!

USUALLY, I **DREAD** THE FIRST DAY OF SCHOOL, BUT **THIS** YEAR IS **DIFFERENT!**

WHY? BECAUSE NOW I'VE GOT A **GIRL-FRIEND!** THAT GIVES ME A **MAJOR** BOOST UP THE SOCIAL LADDER!

WHEN YOU'RE PART OF A COUPLE, YOU BE-COME MORE POPULAR! JUST THINK OF WHAT GOING STEADY WITH ANGIE WILL DO FOR MY REPUTATION!

THINK OF WHAT IT'LL DO FOR **HERS.**

EXACTLY! LIKE DAT-ING **ME** ISN'T **ENOUGH** OF A FRINGE BENEFIT!

YOU'VE GOT MR. ROSA... I'VE GOT MRS. GODFREY.

DANG! WE'RE IN DIFFERENT HOMEROOMS!

THAT MEANS WE'LL ONLY SEE EACH OTHER DURING RECESS AND LUNCH!

WAIT! MAYBE THERE'S A SIMPLE SOLUTION!

YOU COULD ASK TO SWITCH INTO MRS. GODFREY'S HOMEROOM!

COMING UP: OUR FIRST FIGHT.

ARE YOU OKAY? YOU LOOK A LITTLE PALE...

HAVE YOU SEEN ALL THE GUYS IN THIS SCHOOL WHO ARE DROOLING OVER ANGIE? IT'S DIS-**GUSTING!**

SHE'S **MY** GIRLFRIEND! BUT THEY WON'T STOP FLIRTING WITH HER! THEY FLOCK AROUND HER LIKE MOTHS TO A FLAME!

IT'S NOT RIGHT! WHY SHOULD ANGIE HAVE TO DEAL WITH SO MANY ANNOYING LOSERS?

YOU'D THINK **ONE** WOULD BE ENOUGH!

RIGHT! I... **HEY!**

MRS. GODFREY, I HAVE A REQUEST. YOU SEE, MY GIRL-FRIEND ANGIE IS IN YOUR HOMEROOM...

I WANT TO MAKE SURE THAT NO OTHER GUYS TRY TO MOVE IN ON MY WOMAN, IF YOU GET MY DRIFT...

...BUT I CAN'T BE A FLY ON THE WALL, SOOooo...

...SO YOU FIGURED YOU'D BE ONE IN THE OINTMENT.

HERE, JUST RECORD YOUR OB-SERVATIONS IN THIS LITTLE BOOK.

NATE, IT SOUNDS LIKE YOU'RE ASKING ME TO SPY ON ANGIE FOR YOU.

SPY? **NO**! PERISH THE THOUGHT!

IT'S JUST THAT... WELL... SHE'S **NEW** HERE! I WANT TO MAKE SURE SHE'S OKAY! I'M THINKING OF **HER**!

HOW VERY NOBLE OF YOU.

EXACTLY! THAT'S ME! NOBLE! LOOKING OUT FOR THE WELFARE OF MY GIRL-FRIEND!

I SUGGEST YOU LOOK OUT FOR IT SOMEWHERE ELSE.

LET'S GO OVER YOUR SEATING PLAN. ANGIE JUST CAN'T THRIVE SITTING NEAR BOYS.

EVER SINCE I STARTED GOING OUT WITH ANGIE, IT'S LIKE...I FEEL ALL **INSECURE** AND STUFF!

I'M ALWAYS WONDERING IF SHE STILL LIKES ME...I GET ALL FREAKED OUT IF SHE TALKS TO OTHER GUYS... AND I SIT AROUND WORRYING THAT SHE'S GONNA **DUMP** ME!

AT WHAT POINT IN A RELATIONSHIP DOES ALL THAT END?

I HAD TO BE HONEST.

NOW THAT I'M GOING STEADY WITH ANGIE, I'M NOT SURE I'LL BE ABLE TO BE ON THE CHESS TEAM ANYMORE!

CHESS IS A GAME OF **WAR!** I'M TOO HAPPY WITH ANGIE TO THINK ABOUT CAPTURING AND ATTACKING! I JUST CAN'T GET **MEAN** ENOUGH ANYMORE!

SPEAKING OF ANGIE, I JUST SAW MARK JAMESON HITTING ON HER IN THE LIBRARY.

CHECK-MATE.

CHESS IS ALSO A GAME OF CUNNING.

HOW'S YOUR REPORT ON PICASSO GOING, NATE?

AWESOME, I MUST SAY!

I'M NOT REALLY THAT CRAZY ABOUT THE GUY'S ARTWORK, BUT THERE'S PLENTY OF **OTHER** STUFF TO WRITE ABOUT!

CHECK OUT MY ROUGH DRAFT!

"PABLO PICASSO: BABE MAGNET."

A GOOD TITLE REALLY SETS A TONE, DON'T YOU THINK?

IF MY ART-WORK LOOKS DIFFERENT THIS YEAR, MR. ROSA, THERE'S A **REASON** FOR IT!

YOU SEE, I HAVE A **GIRLFRIEND** NOW! OBVIOUSLY, THAT'S CHANGED THE WAY I LOOK AT THE WORLD!

I HAVE A MORE POSITIVE VIEWPOINT! MY ART NOW REFLECTS A MORE CONTENTED PHILOSOPHY!

SO THAT'S WHY ALL THOSE MAGGOTS ARE PINK?

CALL ME MISTER SENSITIVITY!

MY ROMANCE NOVEL, "BELLES-A-POPPIN': A TALE OF LUST AND LOSS IN THE DEEP SOUTH," IS GONNA BE A BEST-SELLER!

BUT WHAT DO **YOU** KNOW ABOUT "LUST AND LOSS"?

MMMF!.. MMMMM

MMMF!.. SMAK

✳ SIIIIIGH...✳

ANY OTHER QUESTIONS?

HERE'S THE SYNOPSIS OF MY ROMANCE NOVEL! THIS WILL GO ON THE BACK COVER!

SET AGAINST THE DRAMATIC BACKDROP OF THE ANTEBELLUM SOUTH, "BELLES-A-POPPIN'" WEAVES A TALE OF TORRID LOVE BETWEEN **VICKI**, A FIERY LOUNGE SINGER, AND **LANCE**, A RUGGED TENNIS PRO!

AS REBEL SOLDIERS DUMP TEA IN THE ATLANTA HARBOR, VICKI FOLLOWS LANCE TO DISNEY WORLD, UNAWARE OF THE WACKY HIGH JINKS WHICH WILL ENSUE DURING A ZANY CHOLERA OUTBREAK!

"WACKY HIGH JINKS"?

CAR CRASHES, FOOD FIGHTS... STUFF LIKE THAT.

ANY ROMANCE NOVEL NEEDS A GOOD **COVER!** ANGIE, YOU AND I WILL POSE WHILE TEDDY TAKES SOME PHOTOS!

I DON'T WANT MY PICTURE ON THE COVER OF SOME BOOK!

IT WON'T BE! I'LL **PAINT** THE COVER! I JUST NEED SOME PHOTOS TO WORK FROM!

ALL THE BEST COVERS SHOW THE GIRL TEARING THE GUY'S SHIRT OFF! ANGIE, YOU GO AHEAD AND RIP MY SHIRT OFF! OOOOH, THIS'LL BE **HOT!**

OW! OW!

DON'T ASK.

I'M READY TO SEND MY ROMANCE NOVEL TO PUBLISHERS! I FINALLY FIGURED OUT HOW TO END IT!

ON THE EVE OF THEIR WEDDING DAY, OUR STAR-CROSSED LOVERS ARE TRAMPLED TO DEATH BY CRAZED BURROS WHILE TOURING THE GRAND CANYON!

SO YOU SEE, THEY'RE TOTALLY **DOOMED!** BEFORE THEIR LOVE CAN BLOOM, IT WITHERS AND DIES ON THE VINE!

A FITTING METAPHOR FOR YOUR LITERARY CAREER.

LATER, THEY COME BACK TO LIFE AS KICK-BOXING ZOMBIES...

RRRRINNNNGGGG

HAND IN THOSE HOME-WORKS, GANG!

OOPS! MISS CLARKE, I JUST REALIZED I DIDN'T WRITE MY NAME ON MY HOME-WORK.

THAT'S OKAY, NATE.

I KNOW YOUR WORK WHEN I SEE IT.

EVER HAVE TROUBLE TELLING A COMPLIMENT FROM AN INSULT?

The Adventures Of...

MOE MENTUM,

★ HOLLYWOOD ★
STUNT MAN!!

On the set of "TITANIC: THE MOVIE".

J.B., we just showed the movie to our test market audience!

Well, what'd they think? Do we have a hit on our hands?

With just a few minor changes, we will! There were a couple of parts the audience didn't like!

Which parts?

Well, they got a little bummed out when the ship actually sank.

I can't stand it...

Also, the whole 1912 thing didn't register. Can we update it to the bikini era?

He's *ACTION-PACKED!*

MOE MENTUM,

☆ ~~Hollywood~~ ☆
STUNT MAN!

On the set of "TITANIC: THE MOVIE."

Folks, we've got a little bit of re-shooting to do.

Test audiences didn't like our ending, so we're going to film another version **WITHOUT** the ship-wreck part!

But won't that make it a totally different film?

Don't do this!

Now, don't panic, people! We're **STILL** making a movie about events aboard a ship at sea!

what KIND of movie?

♪ LOVE.... exciting and new... ♫

HI! I'm Isaac, your bar-tender!

Let's try to make the best of it, gang...

WHAT'S ALL THIS?

JUST GETTING READY FOR HALLOWEEN.

WHOA, **WHOA!** YOU CAN'T HAND OUT THIS STUFF! THIS ISN'T EVEN **REAL CANDY!** IT'S THAT LAME **GENERIC** STUFF!

NATE, CANDY'S CANDY. BESIDES, BUYING THAT KIND SAVED ME ALMOST FIVE DOLLARS.

ADD MY HOUSE TO THE "EGG LIST."

HERE, DAD. I WANT YOU TO HAND OUT COPIES OF THIS DIS-CLAIMER ON HALLOWEEN.

IT SAYS THAT EVEN THOUGH YOU, DAD, ARE GIVING OUT GENERIC CANDY, **I**, NATE, HAD ABSOLUTELY NOTHING TO DO WITH THIS SHAMEFUL DECISION!

AFTER ALL, I'VE GOT TO PROTECT MY REPU-TATION!

YOU MIS-SPELLED FOUR WORDS IN THE FIRST SEN-TENCE ALONE.

I DID?

I'D SAY YOUR REP-UTATION'S INTACT!

LOOK AT THAT, WILL YOU? NONE OF THE TRICK-OR-TREATERS IS EVEN BOTHERING TO GO TO MY HOUSE!

OBVIOUSLY THE WORD IS OUT THAT MY DAD IS HANDING OUT LAME GENERIC CANDY! I **TOLD** HIM THIS WOULD HAPPEN!

NOBODY WANTS TO EAT THAT AWFUL STUFF! **NOBODY!**

☼ BURP ☼

MRS. GODFREY IS SUCH A **SOCIOPATH**! TODAY SHE—

NATE! **NATE!**

YOU PUT ME IN A VERY AWKWARD POSITION WHEN YOU GOSSIP ABOUT MY FELLOW TEACHERS! I DON'T WANT TO HEAR IT!

OKAY, MR. ROSA, I GOTCHA. FROM NOW ON, I'LL REFER TO HER SIMPLY AS "MADAME X."

I APPRECIATE YOUR DISCRETION.

ANYWAY, I'M FLIPPING THROUGH MADAME X'S DAY PLANNER, WHEN SUDDENLY...

... AND SO IT TURNED OUT THAT **ANGIE** HAD PAINTED THIS AMAZ-ING PAINTING! MY **GIRLFRIEND** IS A BETTER ARTIST THAN **I** AM!

AND YOUR EGO CAN'T TAKE IT, EH?

OH, DON'T GIVE ME THAT! THIS HAS NOTHING TO DO WITH MY **EGO**!

MY EGO IS JUST **FINE**, THANK YOU! FOR YOUR INFORMATION, I HAP-PEN TO HAVE ONE OF THE **BEST** EGOS AROUND!

THANKS FOR CLEARING THAT UP.

I'LL JUST HAVE TO BREAK UP WITH HER, THAT'S ALL.

SO YOUR GIRLFRIEND DID A BEAUTIFUL PAINTING! WHY ARE YOU ACTING SO **COMPETITIVE** ABOUT IT?

DOESN'T IT MAKE **SENSE** THAT SHE'LL DO SOME THINGS BETTER THAN YOU?

YEAH, BUT WHERE DOES IT END?

SUPPOSE SHE'S **SMARTER** THAN ME! OR MORE POPULAR! OR A BETTER ATHLETE!

THE CUTE PART IS, HE THINKS HE'S BEING HYPO-THETICAL.

WHY AREN'T YOU SAYING ANY-THING?

UH... ANGIE?

HI, NATE!

ANGIE, I...UH... NEVER REALLY TOLD YOU YESTERDAY HOW MUCH I LIKE YOUR PAINTING.

IT'S GREAT!... NO, IT'S **BETTER** THAN GREAT! IT'S A **MASTER-PIECE!**

THAT'S SO SWEET!

SO YOU THINK THAT REALLY LOOKS LIKE ELVIS?

OH, YEAH. YOU DID AN **AMAZ-ING** JOB ON THE SEQUINS!

137

...SO AT FIRST, I FELT A LITTLE **JEALOUS** THAT YOU'D DONE SUCH AN AWESOME PAINTING!

BUT FRANCIS HELPED ME SEE THAT SUCH A COMPETITIVE ATTITUDE ISN'T HEALTHY! NOW, I CAN ACCEPT THE FACT THAT WE'RE **BOTH** GOOD ARTISTS!

THAT'S GREAT, NATE! I'M GLAD!

SO, WANNA GO DO SOMETHING? WANNA PLAY CHESS?

UM... NOT REALLY.

MONOPOLY?

NO

YAHTZEE?

NO

WANNA THUMB-WRESTLE?

...SO THEN WHEN I GAVE MR. STAPLES THE DRAWING I'D DONE OF HIM, HE DIDN'T EVEN **CARE** THAT I HADN'T DONE MY HOMEWORK!

YOU SEE WHAT THIS **MEANS**? I'LL DRAW CARICATURES OF **ALL** THE TEACHERS! I MAY **NEVER** HAVE TO DO ANOTHER HOMEWORK ASSIGNMENT!

OF COURSE, I'VE GOT TO MAKE SURE THEY **LIKE** THE DRAWINGS! NOTHING LIKE A LITTLE FLATTERY, I ALWAYS SAY!

THINK THAT LOOKS LIKE MR. GALVIN?

THE HALO MIGHT BE A BIT MUCH.

AARGH!

WHAT ARE YOU **DOING**?

I'M TRYING TO DRAW A CARICATURE OF MISS CLARKE, BUT I CAN'T GET IT RIGHT! I'VE BEEN WORKING ON IT FOR **TWO HOURS!**

IT'LL ALL BE WORTH IT, THOUGH! WHEN I GIVE THIS TO HER, I'LL GET OUT OF DOING THE HOMEWORK!

THIS SOUNDS LIKE BRIBERY.

BRIBERY? FRANCIS! YOU **WOUND** ME!

THAT'S NOT A BAD IDEA.

WELL, IT TOOK ALL NIGHT, BUT I DID CARICATURES OF **ALL** OUR TEACHERS! THIS COULD LAND ME ON THE **HONOR ROLL!**

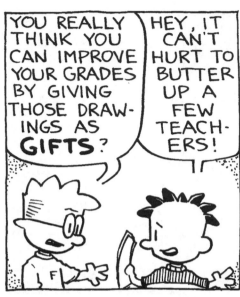

YOU REALLY THINK YOU CAN IMPROVE YOUR GRADES BY GIVING THOSE DRAWINGS AS **GIFTS**?

HEY, IT CAN'T HURT TO BUTTER UP A FEW TEACHERS!

YOU CALL IT BUTTERING UP. **I** CALL IT CHEATING!

FRANCIS, **PLEASE!** "CHEAT" IS SUCH AN **UGLY** WORD!

YES, I KNOW.

SPEAKING OF UGLY, YOU KNOW HOW HARD IT WAS TO DO A FLATTERING DRAWING OF MRS. GODFREY?

HELLO, NATE! READY FOR ANOTHER GREAT HOOPS SEASON?

YOU BET, COACH!

I'M GOING TO BE A DIFFERENT PLAYER THIS YEAR! A LOT MORE **AGGRESSIVE!**

I'M GOING TO TAKE SOME OF THE TECHNIQUES I'VE LEARNED IN **OTHER** SPORTS AND APPLY THEM TO **BASKETBALL!**

YES, I SEE YOU'RE WEARING CLEATS.

WELL, I COULDN'T FIND ANY GOLF SPIKES THAT FIT ME...

NAB!

VETO!

YOU KNOW, THAT TRAMPOLINE WON'T BE THERE DUR-ING ACTUAL GAMES.

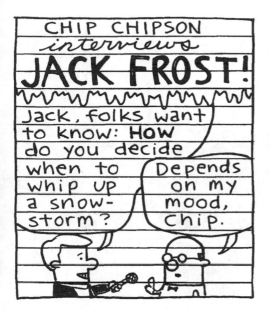

FRANCIS! HEY, GUESS WHAT? MY DAD SAID IT'S OKAY! I'M GONNA HAVE A PARTY!

YEAH, THIS IS GONNA BE THE BASH OF THE CENTURY! I CAN'T WAIT TO START MAKING PLANS!

I'LL HAVE THE BEST DECORATIONS!... THE BEST FOOD!... THE BEST MUSIC!

I FOUND MY SING-ALONG STUFF!

ACTUALLY, LET ME GET BACK TO YOU ON THE MUSIC...

WHAT ARE YOU DOING?

TAKING DOWN THESE PICTURES YOU'VE GOT HANGING EVERYWHERE.

DURING THIS PARTY, ALL MY CLASSMATES WILL BE HERE! YOU THINK I WANT THEM SEEING GOOFY BABY PICTURES OF ME WEARING A DIAPER?

NOW, NATE, I REALLY THINK YOU'RE OVER~

HERE'S A FEW MORE TO GET RID OF.

THESE ARE OF YOUR SISTER.

IT'S A PARTY, NOT A FREAK SHOW. YOU WANT TO LOSE THOSE PERMANENTLY, BE MY GUEST.

WHAT IS **WITH** YOU? YOUR PARTY'S ABOUT TO START AND ALL YOU CAN DO IS **EAT**!

I CAN'T HELP IT! I EAT WHEN I GET NERVOUS!

THIS IS THE FIRST PARTY WHERE I'LL BE PART OF A **COUPLE**! I'M STRESSIN' OUT! I DON'T KNOW WHAT TO DO! AM I SUPPOSED TO MAKE OUT WITH ANGIE OR **WHAT**?

AND IF I **AM**, HOW DO I **DO** IT? WHAT DO I DO FIRST?

DING DONG!

PRETTY MUCH THE EXACT OPPOSITE OF WHAT YOU'RE DOING NOW.

CHOMP! NARF NARF

WELL, NATE, ALL YOUR FRIENDS SEEM TO BE HAVING A GOOD TIME! YOU'VE PUT ON A GREAT PARTY!

OOP! WAS THAT THE DOORBELL? BETTER GO CHECK IT OUT!

NOW... WHERE WERE WE?

ANGIE, YOUR MOM'S HERE TO PICK YOU UP.

NO!

Hello again, friends... I'm Biff Biffwell. Tonight on "Up Close And Personal," we focus on a man who truly exemplifies this joyous time of year: SANTA CLAUS!

Santa is adored by millions, but he remains a **mysterious** figure! As you might expect, he declined to be interviewed for this story.

FILE PHOTO

So instead, we've assembled a portrait of the man **BEHIND** the myth! We've spoken with dozens of people who knew him **BEFORE** he achieved worldwide fame!

Yes, tonight we bring you...

SANTA: UNCOVERED!

The crushed-velvet pantsuit didn't bother me... but when he started hanging out with elves... well...

Santa's Mother

cont'd

SANTA: UNCOVERED!!

Years before he became an international star, Santa was just a normal kid! **EDDIE MACGREGOR** was Santa's best friend!

To me, he was always "Nick."

He liked to play ball, go fishing, stuff like that! There was never even the slightest hint that he'd be famous one day!

But then, when he started to hit the big time... well, you could see it happening! He got conceited! Success started to go to his head!

When did you realize things had changed? When he put that "Saint" in front of his name. That tipped me off.

cont'd!

SANTA: UNCOVERED!

A shocking revelation from Santa's past: He divorced his first wife!

At first, we were happy...

...But then, I began to suspect he was leading a **double life**! I knew him as "Nick", but then he started getting mail addressed to "Kris Kringle"! Our marriage couldn't stand the strain!

I'll tell you one thing, though: If I'd known he was going to become such a big shot, I NEVER would have signed that prenup!

Pre-nup?

Four lumps of coal and a fruitcake per month! Like I'm supposed to LIVE on that!

ABOUT THE AUTHOR

Lincoln Peirce has been drawing the *Big Nate* comic strip for more than 20 years. Born in Ames, Iowa, Peirce grew up in Durham, New Hampshire. As a kid, he began creating his own strips in the sixth grade. Peirce taught high school in New York City and has created several animated pilots for Cartoon Network and Nickelodeon. He lives in Portland, Maine, with his family.

Andrews McMeel Publishing
a division of Andrews McMeel Universal
1130 Walnut Street, Kansas City, Missouri 64106

www.andrewsmcmeel.com

15 16 17 18 19 RR2 10 9 8 7 6 5 4 3 2

ISBN: 978-1-4494-7281-8

Big Nate can be viewed on the Internet at
www.gocomics.com/big_nate

ATTENTION: SCHOOLS AND BUSINESSES
Andrews McMeel books are available at quantity discounts with bulk purchase for educational, business, or sales promotional use. For information, please e-mail the Andrews McMeel Publishing Special Sales Department:
specialsales@amuniversal.com.

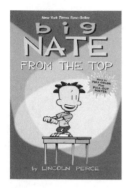   

 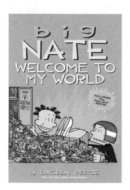